"One who reaches the inner depths of oneself fined true peace".

Become Enlightened

"The gateway of peace remains silent".

Become Enlightened

"One who sees all knows many".

Become enlightened

"The Soul is full many treasure one can only inherent through peace".

Become Enlightened

"Finding your peace is to finding your path."

Become Enlightened

"The Righteous one is the offspring of Wisdom".

Become Enlightened

"True wealth is knowing when to let go."

Become Enlightened

"Fire is not the enemy of water they are just mirrors of one another."

Become Enlightened

"Emotions are jewels to keep well-polished with self-control."

Become Enlightened

"Peace is the freedom of all things."

Become Enlightened

"Love is the gate that opens and never shut."

Become Enlightened

"Become wiser with truth she behold all possibilities."

Become Enlightened

"Justice is the beauty of freedom."

Become Enlightened

"Open what is closed in the heart and the mind shall reward you."

Become Enlightened

"There is no trouble in peace she prevails righteously."

Become Enlightened

"Find your mark on the mountain of love."

Become Enlightened

"True desires are friendly to the soul, but a blessing is born out of peace."

Become Enlightened

"Every righteous deed is a seed in the garden of life."

Become Enlightened

"Eliminate distress by accepting peace as she is."

Become Enlightened

"One shall seek victory before the battle even occur."

Become Enlightened

"The most satisfying thing one can do is to love what has already been done."

Become Enlightened

"To stimulate love you must first kiss peace."

Become Enlightened

"If you wish to find gold never dig in the earth but in one's own soul."

Become Enlightened

"Glorify not you own deeds but the need to give more."

Become Enlightened

"It is wise to see a child filled with joy than a mother filled with sorrow."

Become Enlightened

"Weak is he who breaks the back of his servant to please his guess."

Become Enlightened

"No soul shall find truth when his heart loves a lie."

Become Enlightened

"Continue to grow is the best advice to give a tree."

Become Enlightened

"Outside is the moon that shines when the forest wolf cries."

Become Enlightened

"Give thanks to the ignorant for teaching you to be wise."

Become Enlightened

"Days are long if you count time but nights are shorter than others."

Become Enlightened

"Keep at will that one day your purpose will be proven to you the day you accept peace."

Become Enlightened

"Like all beings of light and darkness your choices are limited by your ignorance to self."

Become Enlightened

"May your journey be wise my friend accept the muddy paths to soften your steps."

Become Enlightened

"Like no other life is only a fruit that never falls from the tree."

Become Enlightened

"Keep in mind that that treasures aren't because they have been left behind."

Become Enlightened

"Life and joy are cousins that are both of your classmates so be happy and make friends."

Become Enlightened

"Create your opportunity to find your destiny."

Become Enlightened

"Open doors that are locked not closed."

Become Enlightened

"Look for a way to stop looking."

Become Enlightened

"Achieve self without effort."

Become Enlightened

"Grow your heart with your mind."

Become Enlightened

"Reach the top while touching the bottom."

Become Enlightened

"Explore the self-who's engraved in richest."

Become Enlightened

"Occupy the one mind and many will be revealed."

Become Enlightened

"Congratulate the ignited soul for she has to bear witness to the end of time."

Become Enlightened

"Knowledge of wisdom is the complete path to finding the mastermind within you."

Become Enlightened

"Don't leave joy to inherit life's sorrows when the truth unravels mysteries."

Become Enlightened

"True love is in the abyss of the soul, where no sees and seems to know."

Become Enlightened

"To become noticeable to the hearts of others, you must surrender your through love."

Become Enlightened

"We find laughter in our lives hoping to become as the wise."

Become Enlightened

"Every soul is wise, the wiser you become the greater your glory."

Become Enlightened

"On the arrival of judgement feel free to take stand and swear under the oath of honor."

Become Enlightened

"There's two ways to accept virtually, one I to remove all baggage and 2 never dumpster dive."

Become Enlightened

"We seem to be innocent when the law is applied to us, but the truth and freedom are one, Love."

Become Enlightened

"Choose your steps as if they were raindrop, stand still and you'll find yourself in a puddle."

Become Enlightened

"Relate to life as if she's your mother giving you a fresh start to love yourself as is."

Become Enlightened

"Do you hope to see the peak of Royalty of your progress, than begin as a servant?"

Become Enlightened

"Life and joy are both like flowers in a garden picking them both satisfy you and your mate."

Become Enlightened

"Just to acknowledge love is to appreciate the divine art of significance and passion both inherited through the self."

Become Enlightened

"Life is the ultimate treasure, so keep your memories polished, make your love well furnished, and share your compassion with many."

Become Enlightened

"Receive what is given to you by love, and do not throw it in the abyss, cling to it for it is a mighty token from above."

Become enlightened

"Fire is never the same when two people are split apart, but it grows the closer you get to your true love."

Become Enlightened

"Indeed what you witness through your eyes are a dream in the world of fantasy, but what you feel inside is the reality of destiny."

Become Enlightened

"True Enlightenment has a breath of truth in every word you speak, so carry the wisdom you receive from it as your very own."

Become Enlightened

Made in the USA
Columbia, SC
14 January 2022

53748969R00037